A Cracked Egg

A story of loss and love to Resilient Overcomer

Carla

Thanks for your Support

Stephanie Rochelle
2019

Stephanie Rochelle

Published by Still Standing Publishing Co.
Cover photo by Rehobath Media

Printed in the United States of America

ISBN 9781091375864

Dedication

This book is dedicated to parents who have lost their child or are learning how to get through their child's illness. Losing my son to a terminal illness, unfortunately, taught me to push through the trials of life. Parents may also suffer the loss of a child due to incarceration or drugs. As a parent, a child unable to enjoy life or a child missing from home is still a devastating loss.

This book is also dedicated to women who have experienced a loss due to divorce. The trials of life sometimes weigh heavily on mothers and we need a way to push through the days ahead and learn to navigate our new normal with daily decisions. These decisions are necessary for transformation.

Daily Decisions

D – Do what makes you happy

E - Everyday

C – Choose to affirm yourself daily

I – I Am

S - Strong

I – I Will

O – Overcome my

N – New Normal with

S – Self Love

Acknowledgements

I would like to acknowledge and thank those individuals in my life who encouraged and supported me through my journey of transformation. My beautiful mom especially, and my totally supportive friends, you know who you are. So thankful I'm blessed to have you all in my life.

Special thanks for my son Ryan who taught me that life is not promised so we must enjoy it and make the best out of every day we have on this earth. To my daughter, Autumn, being blessed with you allowed me to be a mom again, the best job on this earth. You truly make us proud. Continue to go after it all, and never stop speaking exactly what you want.

To my husband, my fairytale, thanks for always believing in me and giving me your love and support. With you, I can let my light shine bright. I'm forever thankful and grateful that we met in 2013. Through you, God also blessed me with Alexis, AJ, and Ari, who I truly love and enjoy being a part of their life.

Introduction

Life's trials can teach you more than you ever wanted to learn sometimes. If you've been hit hard by life or if you've experienced a devastating loss due to illness, incarceration, drugs or divorce, this book will support you in a few ways to overcome the struggles of life by resetting your emotions and practicing self-care daily.

Even through my pain, I was always the girlfriend that if asked, had a true word to give. I offered words of encouragement and support. Writing this book was painful. It forced me to relive each and every trial. The feeling of accomplishment that came from writing this self-help book was well worth it.

Are you stuck or experiencing a toxic relationship, depression, fear, failure, loss, or divorce? If so, your life represents a cracked egg and needs to be rebuilt from the inside out. After losing my son to cancer, I had to rebuild my life. After giving birth to my daughter, I had to rebuild my life again without fear of losing another child. After going through a lengthy divorce, I rebuilt my life as a single parent learning to live in my new normal. Taking the steps to rebuild my life allowed me to bounce back with a strong foundation.

I pray my journey to transformation supports you and affirms that if you're open and teachable, you can be an overcomer. I've dedicated myself to helping women who are stuck, find power in their pain so they can move forward with renewed clarity, mindset, confidence, and fearless determination so they can live their fairytale life and win at love and business. Everything we go through we can use to help others through their journey. Fear keeps us captive, but everything we want in life is on the other side of fear.

Do you believe in fairytales? After all the pain, I met my prince, and we are living out our fairytale. Beyond the pain a beautiful life was waiting in the wings for me to grab and have the ending I always wanted. Just as God said, I got everything I wanted.

Contents

Chapter 1
Who am I?

As kids, we don't always realize how our experiences both good and bad shape our lives. You start out with a blank slate, and as life happens, it chips away and forms who you become. I've learned you don't have to remain a cracked egg.

April Fools 1992, I get an unexpected call. "He's gone." Huh, whose gone?" Grandpa died today." Is this a joke. I thought, but of course not. It was so ironic to lose my favorite guy on April Fool's day, unexpectantly.

Meek, mild but full of strength was my grandma. "Grandma, how are you holding up?"

She smiled which I assumed meant she was in disbelief.

Let me back up. My childhood was a bed of roses. I was born in August 1966, in the small town of Warren, Ohio. My parents divorced when I was five, and Mom and I went to live with my grandparents until she figured out what was next. My grandparents had a huge, white house in the country. The home sat on their own personal lake with a circular driveway and a three-car garage. It had a garden as long as a driveway and a swimming pool for the grandkids. Mom and I lived upstairs. We had two bedrooms, a kitchen, a dining room, and a family room with a piano that none of the grandkids played.

You see, what seemed awesome to outsiders was simply normal to me. All I knew was, I was in heaven living with my two most favorite people, until mom saved for our house.

Each morning I ran down the spiral staircase without stopping, until I reached the kitchen where grandpa sat waiting on me for breakfast. He ate a full breakfast while reading his paper, and I ate oatmeal. Grandma stood there looking at us with her hands on her hips watching to make sure we both had everything we needed.

Grandpa went off to work at the cleaners, and I went off to school. Again, just a normal day. I didn't realize how my life was forming. As I write, I smile. My grandpa was the owner of Johnson Cleaners. The first and only black person in Warren to own and operate a dry cleaners. Everyone knew my family. My grandma didn't work or drive. She took care of us.

I was raised to be respectful and smile at everyone I met. She would say everyone deserves a smile, and it might be just what they need that day. I was young, and didn't quite understand what she meant, nevertheless, my grandma said it, so it's the gospel. She showed me what it was like to take care of a family. There were four grandchildren, and we all hung out at our grandparent's house. Childhood days included strawberry picking, pool parties, and ice skating on the lake in the winter months. Years passed. Mom and I moved to our own home. The grandkids became teenagers, and all of us, except for my baby cousin, worked at the cleaners. Three girls and one boy. My boy cousin actually got to learn the family business including how to operate and run the machines. The girls ran the front. Girls were not allowed, I guess, to work in the back doing manual labor. We were customer service.

Aha moment:

In writing this I smile. I had the best childhood anyone can ask for, filled with loads of love and support.

My grandpa was our view of entrepreneurship, customer service, and respect.

Chapter 2

A Season of Pain

I graduated high school, left for college, but halfway through college married my high school sweetheart and moved to Florida. Both of us were Ohio natives. My husband was in the US Navy and stationed in Florida. Our journey begins. Let's see what Florida had to offer.

Timing is everything. After graduating college one month later, I had our son. Once I became a mom, I wanted to be closer to family, so we moved to Atlanta. It wasn't Ohio, but we had family and friends there, so it was an easy choice.

Getting married so young and then having a child, I didn't know how to be a wife or mother, so I emulated the couple I saw growing up, my grandparents. I took care of my family the same way my grandmother took care of me. I made sure they were well. It was my job to make sure they had what they needed.

Atlanta was known to be great for the black and educated. We had good jobs, and decided we were there to stay, so we bought a house.

Life was great, or so we thought, but something didn't seem quite right with our son. His balance was off. I took him to several doctors, and everything kept checking out, but still his balance was off. After taking him back to his pediatrician, because I was frustrated and needed answers. She watched him walk up and down her hallway and decided to send him for one more test. No parent ever really thinks anything is wrong with their child. Maybe he needs this, maybe he needs that. We were casually sitting in the waiting room waiting on the doctor to come back and tell us our next steps. We expected to hear a simple explanation of what was wrong and what we needed to do next.

However, it went way different than expected. The doctor came into the waiting room and point blank said our son had a brain tumor and it was wrapped around his brain stem. He was so cold and emotionless. My husband and I were in disbelief. One day my son was playing outside and a little wobbly, and the next day, he had a brain tumor. That day in October 1994, changed our lives forever.

"A brain tumor? Isn't that cancer?' I could barely say the word, still processing that it was my two-year-old son we we're talking about. The doctor gave us an appointment card to come back in the next Monday to discuss our course of action.

Course of action? He's two.

"Ma'am, your son is very sick," the doctor said.

The ride home was so quiet. I felt like I should scream or at least cry, but nothing would come out. As parents, we were terrified. The next Tuesday, we were set to start his first round of chemotherapy.

When you have chemo or have to return for several treatments, they insert a shunt, so you won't have to get stuck every time you have an appointment. Ryan endured months of treatment like a champ. Whether we were in denial or not, his scar on the back of his head was our proof that he was indeed sick. I hoped he would take his treatment, we would thank God for his recovery, and he could go back to being a kid. Unfortunately, our son was still fighting for his life 8 months later. The tumor shrank but was still wrapped around his brain stem.

The hardest test a parent faces is something happening to their child and there's nothing anyone can do. All I knew to do was pray and ask God for help. Whether I wanted it to be or not, this was our appointed journey. A season of pain.

I loved on him constantly and was there for every step of his journey. I wanted his life to be as happy and as normal as possible. He wanted to be like his friends and play soccer and T-ball. The fun times didn't last. It became time to address the next course of action to kill the rest of the tumor wrapped around his brain stem. The doctors wanted to start radiation.

Ryan, age three, was such a happy kid. He would surely beat cancer. Each month after treatment, he'd say "Time for school, Mommy." It broke my heart. He just wanted to be normal.

I didn't know anyone who lost their child, so the entire time he went for treatments, I held on to the hope that kids never died before their parents. Hope and my faith in God was all I had. It got me through having a kid with a brain tumor. Treatment after treatment, we both became sick of the hospital and were ready to have fun.

Aha moment:

In writing this, I realized where my strength came from. My adult life I emulated my grandma. How she took care of me growing up was how I took care of my family. I felt like it was my job to make sure they had everything they needed.

Life scripture: Hebrews 11:1
Now faith is the substance of things hoped for, the evidence of things not seen.

Chapter 3
Foundation of Faith

The radiation treatments were complete. Was our son cancer free? Would we get to ring the bell? Again, we didn't get the news we hoped for. The radiation didn't work, either. That stubborn cancer was still wrapped around his brain stem, and unfortunately once you had radiation you couldn't get it again in the same spot. We came to the end of our journey, and it didn't end the way we hoped. There was nothing else they could do. Eventually his body started shutting down.

I kept saying, he's four-years-old. They asked us to sign a DNR, Do Not Resuscitate. Hospice care was the next step. They asked if we wanted him to go through hospice from home or from a facility. I said, home, of course.

As we pulled out the hospital parking deck, I swear, Ryan died in the back seat. I prayed and shouted at God please don't take our son. God spared his life, and he came back. Children are a gift from God, and he loans them to us for a period of time that only God knows. I never thought it would be only four years.

Another quiet ride home, full of tears. I kept looking at Ryan in the back seat asking God "please don't take my son." I continued to believe God would send a miracle. A miracle was the only way our child would live. This is a child who hadn't hurt anyone. I expected him to get a chance to become a productive adult. Why would we have to lose our child? I always did the right thing and treated people right, just like I was raised to do. Why does my child have to die? That is the hardest test in trusting that God knows best, but how could God's plan for Ryan's life, be that?

Month's passed, until one day I noticed he wasn't having a good day. His breathing was shallow. I got scared and called 911. The first question they asked was do we have a DNR. Before I knew it, I said no. I wanted God to save my baby, I expected him to.

I was screaming and crying, talking to Ryan, "Don't leave me." He was tired. He shook his head as to say, 'No mom, I've had enough." I think God knew that I couldn't take anymore either. I wanted to be selfish. I wanted my son to live at any cost. As his mom, I didn't want to see him suffer. Once we reached the hospital, they found out we indeed had a DNR, so they stopped all attempts to save him and within less than 30 minutes they called his time of death. His dad was on the way, but it was too late. It was time to say goodbye.

The medical staff asked if we wanted to donate his organs. With his spirit, I smiled at the thought of him helping someone have what he always wanted. A normal life. I consented to donate his organs.

For our final viewing, I had no idea how I would react when we saw his body. My husband and I arrived at the funeral home and got the biggest blessing ever. We walked into the room, approached the casket, and to our surprise he lay there with what looked like the biggest smile of peace on his face. The look of freedom. He was now healed. Not the way we expected, but now he was free of pain.

Journal About Disappointment

How do you deal with disappointment when things don't go the way you hoped and prayed?

_____

_____

_____

_____

If things didn't go the way you wished, but you needed to be happy and keep a smile on your face for your dying child—how would you do that?

_____

_____

_____

Being the best mom to him, I was his uplift and support, because I was there and made sure he was okay. I received solace and comfort in my grief process. I fulfilled my job. As for my husband, we never really talked about losing our son. He wasn't there for me, and I wasn't there for him. We tried to rebuild our lives after experiencing the most traumatic experience ever in our lives.

I spoke to my husband about us going to counseling. This time rebuilding our life took the both of us. He didn't think we needed it. So, we continued on with living our life.

We booked a trip to Hawaii to visit friends that were stationed there. My best friend was just what I needed. I needed a hug.

Do you have someone to lean on through your trials? Who?

_____

_____

_____

_____

When you are emotionally unavailable, and your spouse is emotionally unavailable, what do you do?

_____

_____

_____

_____

Chapter 4
Reset Emotions

After losing Ryan, my faith took a tumble. Friends stopped by to check on me trying to see if there was anything they could do. I wanted them there, but no one knew what to say. One friend started cleaning up. I appreciated them just being there. Another friend stopped by and put it all in perspective. It's funny how you work with someone and think you know them or know about their life, and then you learn differently. She shared with me her story of loss. She told me to appreciate the four years God gave me. She lost a daughter at just three weeks old. It was just what I needed to hear. Even in your pain, God is still there and will send what you need.

I was filled with anger and mad at God. For a while I wouldn't go to church, even though I knew God didn't make mistakes. During my grief, I couldn't see it. Why did he take my son? We missed out on the rest of his life, seeing him graduate from kindergarten, play sports, and become an adult. A parent's wish is to see what their child becomes.

At church, they preached about healing and miracles, and my son didn't get healed nor did we get a miracle, or so I thought. The fact that my son was happy and ready to go to school as I mentioned before, was my miracle. He never acted sick. He never gave in to the disease. He pushed through. He wanted to live. It just wasn't God's plan. Why was he the sacrifice? The best job in life is being a mother. I knew he belonged to God, but you let everyone else keep their blessing. Why'd you have to take mine?

The stages of grief are different for everybody. For me, during his illness, I stayed in shock, denial, and bargained as his mom. When we lost him, frustration and anger filled my space.

I had good and bad days. Being a mom fills you with emotions on a daily basis. My days became filled with sorrow. I was typically a happy person. I'm not sure if I was depressed but being sad all the time no matter what happened isn't what Ryan would have wanted. In that state, it was very easy to turn to alcohol or something else to ease the pain. This was not an option for me, I had to come up with a way on my bad days to not lose my entire day to sadness. I knew it was normal to be sad, I just wouldn't give into it all day. On days like that, I decided to *Hit Reset*. I reset my emotions. I replaced my thoughts of sadness with thoughts of happy moments with my son. Thoughts that made my heart smile.

Another one of my healing methods was to speak life each and every day. I would start my day with positive affirmations and kept busy playing tennis. I filled my days and nights with whatever made me feel good or smile. I developed a self-care regimen. I got my nails done, hung out with friends, went dancing and read a plethora of books to strengthen my mindset.

I used mindset strategies and my reset method to rebuild my life. Mindset strategies are learned methods or things you do daily that continue to add value to your life and propel you forward.

How do you rebuild your life after losing the love of your life, your child?

The hardest thing to be during that time of loss was positive, but that's exactly what I needed to be. It takes less energy to be happy than it does to be sad.

Ways to Reset your Emotions

1. Reset your thoughts with happy memories, or happy moments with the person you lost.
2. Think about things about them that make you smile or laugh.
3. Dance. Music is a great way to reset your emotions.
4. Fill your space or time with a vigorous activity. For me it was tennis.
5. Learn to meditate and pray. Ask God to help you change your thoughts.
6. Throughout your day, play gospel music in your ear and/or listen to church sermons. Even though I was mad, gospel music had a way of making me feel better. My faith was being restored one song at a time.

Chapter 5
Overcoming FEAR

When you lose a child to a disease that you can't explain or accept, to plan to have another child seemed crazy. Was I setting myself up for the unknown?

Memories of another mother at the hospital flood my mind. She had three children that had cancer. I believe it was kidney cancer. It let me know, sometimes terrible things in life just happen, and it wasn't worth the risk.

Ryan was my first born and could not be replaced. People meant well, but I was speechless when they said just have another child. There's nothing like your first and for him to be taken with a terminal illness, the feelings of fear were real. I pushed through with my strategies and was finally enjoying life again. But my family and friends kept suggesting I do the crazy thing I feared.

I now found myself evaluating the risk. My grandma's daily prayer included asking God to soften my heart, so I would try again. She knew I was mad at God. But I soon found myself talking to and praying to God about my fear. I missed being a mom so much. Maybe having another would help me accept Gods plan. I had to reset my fear before trying for our next child. Using my strategies worked to push through the pain of losing my son, but this next step was harder than losing my son.

I replaced my thoughts of worry and fear and focused on the joy and happiness that being a mom brought me. What would having a healthy child look like? I began speaking good things into my life. Being a mom again, my husband and I rebuilding our life as parents, and finally smiling again.

It was September 1998 when she arrived, and we we're parents again. She was perfect. I appreciated God blessing us with Ryan, but when you lose a child, you really appreciate it all the more.

I continued to grow into my new phase of life making time for family along with time for myself. Continuing to practice my strategies of self-care even though life was good, kept me in a positive mindset.

It seems strange, but after having a sick child, I got to see what it was like to raise a healthy child. I had feelings of completion. With my son only living to age four, I then felt like I would get to see other phases of life through being her mom. God willing. I would have a child that graduated from kindergarten, played sports like softball and tennis, danced in recitals, and attended her 8th grade dance.

Life seemed to be going fine. I had a great job, but my husband and I talked about me quitting my corporate career and pursuing a real estate career full-time. I loved selling homes and helping others. It took some prayer, but I decided to do just that. I figured why not? We'd been married forever, I had always worked and did my part. It was my time to shine and do something that I absolutely loved.

I was nervous. I always worked a corporate job, however, it was the perfect time to take this chance. Financially, he said we were okay. My husband was doing well flipping houses, and I made rookie of the year my first year in real estate.

About a year into us being entrepreneurs, life got stressful. We argued all the time about money. I thought we were okay. As usual, everything that went wrong was my fault. During arguments he started saying he didn't tell me to quit my job. With a look of confusion on my face I said, we were in agreement. I wouldn't just quit a job that I worked for twenty plus years without us being in agreement.

A year or so went by, and we were in a crazy space due to financial stress, or that's what I thought our problem was. Being married as long as we were, there were times of like and times of love. When he wasn't happy, nobody could be happy. He began talking down to me. I started to look for a job. Still thinking our problem was finances. How does a person disrespect someone because of financial problems that he too created? Classic.

What was I thinking? This was the person, that never saw anything he did. Selfish people are just that. Selfish! They don't think they need to change anything, it's how they always have been.

I was tired of him and obviously he was tired of me. Nothing I did was ever good enough. I gave 110% he wanted 125% but never gave it in return. I continued to try to take care of my family. I thought this was just a rough patch. Hell, we made it through much worse. Finally I got the call. A job had opened up at my previous employer. Through the years, after all we'd been through, I asked him if he thought we should go to counseling. We went through a lot and just didn't seem like we were in sync and working to pull our life back together after the financial turmoil.

I tried talking. He said I was pushy. Bills were coming due, even though I was working again I started asking, where was the money from the night job? He was full of excuses. When I arrived at work on Monday, my friend pulled me to the side and asked why I didn't tell him me and my husband were having problems. I asked what he meant. He said my husband brought a lady friend to a party he was attending, and all their wives were looking for me to come through the door and in came someone else. It now became clear that our marriage was in real trouble. Someone who I have always trusted has went to great lengths to make someone else happy or was he really that bold and thought that no one would tell me. Well, my co-worker didn't have a choice to tell me, if he didn't his wife would. Just like my husband thought the brotherhood would keep his secret.

The sisterhood was about to spill the beans. I'm not sure how I did it but I didn't say anything the entire day to my husband. While at work I was just processing all the deceit. How did he pull this off?

I was walking around in a fog the entire day. I had never questioned his whereabouts or whatever he said. If you're a praying wife, everything that happens in the dark will eventually come to light. I finally, arrived home. Something led me to the computer to check my email, and there it was, everything I needed to know and had questions about, he had left his email up. I said, look at God, and I went searching. I needed all the truth, and at this point, he was a liar. I found all kinds of emails. Emails stating that when we divorced, he would marry one of his women.

Yes, he had several according to the emails. One of his women, over the years I asked about her, she was described as one of his business partners for flipping houses. The other actually stayed in our same neighborhood. I had asked about her because I saw his car over their a few times, he stated he was helping her with a few odds and ends. He knew everyone because he was the HOA president for our community. He also had a lawn care business. I always wondered how he was able to still take golf trips and we were in a financial bind. According to the emails, his women had paid for and attended some of his golf trips. Now, he agrees to go to counseling, however, I don't know why.

We went to one session. I didn't really know what I wanted to happen from going to counseling, but it only works when both want to save the marriage. He seemed to use it to point out what was wrong with me. Classic manipulator. There was no need to go to counseling, and there was no need to draw this out. He left the marriage years ago. I just didn't know it. The one thing I got from going to that one session and that I live by and carry with me always is, Love does not hurt.

It was the most humiliating experience to sit and watch my own life play out. I just watched along with everyone else as I prayed for strength to follow through with my next steps—steps he never thought I was strong enough to take. Nine months later, I filed for divorce.

What I knew was he grew up seeing his mom stay with his dad no matter what and thought I would do that same or at least try to hold on.

I waited until my head was clear and I knew I could see it through to finish. I was determined to keep it classy no matter what he did and said to me. I didn't want anybody that didn't want me, so it wasn't that hard. Mindset strategies were on full power and at maximum effectiveness. He didn't know about my reset method nor my mindset routine that I began when our son was sick.

My prayers, daily rituals, choices, personal developments and speaking positive affirmations to myself and over my life, helped me get back to me.

I needed all the strength I built up. I actually thought because he moved on and didn't want our life anymore that once I got myself strong enough to go through with it, he would surely sign the papers. Nope, he prolonged our divorce for a year.

He made excuse after excuse. Every time we went to court, he asked for another extension. One day while driving down the highway, the tears just wouldn't stop. I wanted the divorce to be over. I clearly heard God say, your going to get everything you're supposed to get. The tears dried instantly. I had never experienced hearing God that clear in my entire life. That is what they mean when they say God will be right on time. It was exactly what I needed to see that through. Every time, it looked crazy, or he would ask for an extension, I remembered what God told me.

Once it was out that I knew about the affairs, the two of them were fighting to see who he would choose. Remember he had told them both when he divorced me that he would marry them. He chose the one across town. That's when I got a call from the one in our neighborhood agreeing to come to court with me, in case I needed to prove infidelity. I actually appreciated her for that, however, even though, I understood it was just because she wasn't chosen. I told her she could have won if we weren't in the same subdivision, but now that the neighbors knew, he wasn't about to be on display as the man who left his family. She was silent and in disbelief but still agreed to help me. She also apologized and told me I was nothing like he described. Go figure.

It was now June, I started divorce proceedings in July of the previous year. Something felt different. When we got to court, we had a different judge, and I knew today was the day. He would see we were trying to get this final for so long and would give me the release I needed. I was smiling from ear to ear. It was over. As God said, I got everything I asked for. The entire time, I kept it classy, I didn't argue or give him what he was looking for. I just trusted what God told me.

Aha moment:

Trust and respect is key to marriage. Lies and disrespect are sure to ruin it, every time. Love does not hurt.

Sometimes in marriage, especially in long marriages, we lose ourselves. We tend to agree to disagree to keep the peace. Your true partner will never stop listening or hearing what you have to say. As you continue to work on yourself to become a better person, they too should be working on themselves to become better. Selfish people never think they have to change, but in reality, we all need to change and grow. If you're the same at 40 as you were at 30, you're full of yourself. I vowed never to lose my identity again. I moved forward as a new version of myself. I'm confident. I'm bold. I was in a great place and excited to see what was next. I was a new version of me.

How would you handle another hard fight for your life? Would you be able to keep it together? Would you be able to keep it classy?

Here's how I did it.

While I was going through my divorce, my church was starting this class called Masterlife. They stated it was about becoming a disciple. Members of the church that completed the last session were in church giving testimonies about how this small group course changed their life. I started thinking maybe I should sign up. They mentioned the class was a six-month course. I clearly heard God telling me to sign up. I had no idea really what this class meant, but it seemed to help them through whatever they were going through, so I signed up. It was the best thing I could have done.

It was there that I learned how to master my life.

It was there I learned to Abide in Christ. To make Christ the center of my life, take him everywhere I go, and seek him for every decision.

It was there I learned to spend time with him daily, which started my morning rituals of praying, talking to him, and sometimes meditating to hear or get an answer I needed.

It was there I learned to memorize Bible verses to have down inside me that I could and would call on to get me through.

It was there I learned how to respond and react differently, to be slow to speak.
This small group that God hand-picked for me, saved my life. It became my comfort zone and all twelve of those ladies became my new friends and support system. We are still friends today.

I started out as a participant in Masterlife to being chosen to be on the core team or board of Masterlife. Most recently I was selected to be one of the coordinators of the ministry.

Each year I got stronger. A few years ago, I asked God to stretch me. I felt like I should be doing more in all aspects of my life, but fear was stopping me.

My favorite scriptures from the course were:

- John 15:5 - "I am the vine; you are the branch. If a man remains in me and I in him, he will bear much fruit; apart from me you can do nothing".
- James 1:19 - Wherefore, my beloved brethren, let every man be swift to hear, slow to speak, slow to wrath;

My 12 Steps to Stop Loving Someone Who Has Already Stopped Loving You

1. Accept that it's over, so you can move forward.
2. Let go of the future you created together. It's now time to close that chapter and create a new beginning.
3. Dismantle the past: Sit in the hurt. Take it in. Look at the amazing moments that you had. Journal about the bad times. Look at all the time you compromised to make it work. Don't stay where love is not being returned.
4. Raise your standards for the next life you're building, so you will attract someone in alignment with where you're going.
5. Take heed of the lessons learned. Don't look at it as a failed marriage but a life lesson, which prepared you for your next blessing.
6. After you gain peace, be open to intentional dating. Open your heart, be vulnerable, and get back in the game.
7. Set boundaries for your old life so you can have a new life.

8. Don't follow him/her on any social media.
9. Determine what you want next.
10. Visualize your new life every day. Make your list.
11. If it's the little things you like, make sure you get it. Same values, trustworthy, communicator, wants a relationship and not a hook up etc.
12. Smile every day.

Chapter 6
Creating Boundaries

I'm 45, a single parent, and divorced. I was a single parent trying to balance my new normal versus my old life. Married nearly 30 years, I knew exactly who I was dealing with, so boundaries had to be set. I knew my ex would assume he still had rights where it pertained to our old life. If I didn't set boundaries, when he came to pick up our daughter on his weekends, he would be in my house like he had rights. I said I would keep it classy not that I would be stupid. I didn't let him in my home. I would send Autumn out to her dads' car.

I began going out with girlfriends. I leaned on my friends a lot during this time. They kept me busy on my free weekends. My friend would call me and say get dressed, we are going out. I love to dance. Dancing put a smile on my face. While we were out, I overheard a friend of a friend talking about playing in a kickball league. I thought that would be a good way to get into a different circle and make new friends. Most of my other friends I played tennis with were also in my old circle. The circle my ex and I shared together. I felt in this growing season I needed a new circle, even though I sincerely have love for them. What they didn't know was that my ex, through the years continued to tell me they were not my real friends. So, a fresh start would eventually show if they were or not. In divorce, friends of both the husband and wife typically choose one to remain friends with. In some cases, our friends chose me, in other cases I assumed they chose my ex if we no longer hung out or if they never tried to join my new life.

Nevertheless, I was having an awesome time and the smile on my face was real. I thought it was time to test the dating waters. I wanted to try something different. I was feeling bold. Online dating seemed like it would be a fun way to meet guys until I figured out what I wanted or needed at this stage of life.

The kickball circle became my safe place to enjoy myself. I could play with them to get out the house, and I could enjoy myself without looking for guys to meet.

After coming in from a good time, I decided to create me a profile on Plenty of Fish (POF). I wasn't really sure how the online scene worked because nobody I was around talked about being online. It didn't matter, I vowed to do something different.

Aha moment:

Ladies, if I can tell you one thing, when you trust and ask God for something be ready for him to bring just that. I never asked for a man with money because in my experience, money can be lost. I asked for a man that loved me and loved my daughter like she was his own. I got exactly what God promised me.

Divorce was another loss I suffered. I'm glad I took the time to invest in making me a better person before dating but most people just jump into the next relationship or hookup before trying to heal the pain of emptiness, fear, and the unknown.

How would you handle dating again after divorce? Start meeting guys as friends. Don't rush into being in a relationship.

_____

_____

_____

How to decide if you are ready to date:

Do you still care about what your ex is doing? If not, it's time to date!

_____

_____

_____

_____

_____

Chapter 7
Winning the Online Fairytale

I created my profile with truth. I said I was old-fashioned and wanted a relationship since the majority of my life I had been a wife. I believed in chivalry and that I was looking to start as friends. This time I wanted him to be a communicator, love my daughter, and have his own relationship with the Lord. I was an adult and assumed at this age if they were looking to date or be in a relationship as their profile stated, that they were an adult, too. No games would need to be played, I assumed.

I met some nice guys, but it seemed they either didn't read my profile that I was looking to meet a guy with old-fashioned values or didn't believe my profile. It seemed everyone was looking to have sex. Nobody was willing to take the time to get to know me or court me.

I was looking for a prince, and so far, I only met frogs. I couldn't play the game the way it was being played so I decided to play by my own rules. I came up with a system that would determine if we were looking for the same things or weed out those for whom it was time to say NEXT.

I was dating with intentions of a relationship. I wasn't dating to hookup and hoping it led to a relationship. I began getting frustrated with the frogs and decided to give it a break. One night when I arrived home, out of habit I looked to see if anyone had clicked on my profile looked like we might be a fit.

One guy that clicked, had kids coming out of his shirt sleeve. It caught my attention, but I wasn't sure it made sense. Autumn was in high school and my preference wouldn't be someone with small kids, age 7 and 8. I didn't believe a relationship with kids still in the house could work. You hear all these issues of blended families, but something made me respond back.

We spoke on the phone for two months just getting to know each other. Most men won't spend that amount of time with you. I finally felt comfortable meeting him, so we met for dinner and then dessert. I know now why he asked so many questions. He already decided that I was what he was looking for before meeting. Meeting in person was just a formality.

Literally our hearts connected over those two months. You heard me say he decided I was it, but I had not decided. So, I say. Even though our hearts connected my heart was guarded. We went on a few dates, then I let him meet my mom and daughter. Autumn had not met any of the men I dated, or she didn't know they were trying to date me.

When Alex arrived at my home, he had gifts. A gift for my daughter (Skittles) and a gift for my mom (a candle). This man was listening while we were talking. He knew what each of them liked. They were hooked. I still kept my guard up. He promised my heart was safe with him. I was scared to trust his love. He literally oozed love, which was so different, I never experienced a man like that, but something different is exactly what I needed. My heart was smiling but I was scared. I started to sabotage it. I would ask, "You seem so nice, why are you divorced?"

He would say he would be the same man six months from now, that this is who he was.

It's funny now, how I almost missed my blessing.

I was looking to buy a car and needed a man's presence, so I asked him to meet me at the dealership. We talked about me meeting his kids, so he decided to bring them with him when he came to the dealership.

Before even becoming a family, we were a family. From that introduction and every other weekend, he had his kids, so we did kid activities. It wasn't until he stopped by and had the kids that I noticed his son, like his dad, took care of us girls and made sure we were okay. That little boy was eight.

Alex toted Autumn wherever she needed to go and be picked up from. She loved it. They formed a bond. We toted Ari and AJ to cheerleading and football. Our family formed.

Our life was something you read about in books, and I thought it was just a dream. It was actually our fairy tale. God had sent the exact person I needed to add value to my and Autumn's life. I thought I found my fairy tale but needed a skeptical but loving point of view.

I knew how to solve that. My cousin was having a retirement party for her husband in North Carolina. I knew there I would find out if what I thought was good was really good for me. Me and my cousin, we are a lot alike, I was curious to see what she thought about my choice for me and my daughter. He made it past Autumn and my mom, but I needed a third eye. An eye like mine.

Most people don't care what others think, but I'm very close to my family and wanted it to be a good fit. My cousins knew I was bringing someone for them to meet, so that meant they would tell me what they thought secretly. They wouldn't mention that they liked him out loud. They wouldn't mention this where he could hear.

They both yelled, don't mess this up. We like him, he responds, she can't mess it up. We continued to date and learn about each other. Then it happened, Alex got laid off. Our first test and trial. His spirit changed. Men that want to support their family and can't, typically shut down or get quiet. We had our first argument. He shut down on me and from previous experience, I knew that didn't work for me. The baggage we carry sometimes creeps in and we don't even realize it.

He searched for jobs, but nothing stuck so he took a job out of town, and I supported him.

It was time for him to leave. We had become partners, soulmates. We went to the dollar store and everywhere together. Now he was gone. Who can get mad at a man that's supporting his family and soon to be wife? For two years he worked out of town and traveled back and forth.

It's funny now, how I almost missed my blessing.

March 2015, he proposed with a fairy tale proposal. Several of our friends planned a trip to go to a concert in Miami. They knew about the proposal. I thought we were traveling and hanging as we usually did. We had a ball. I knew nothing. We all came from Atlanta except my cousins in North Carolina and Alex came in from Texas where he was working.

I got a little irritated at Alex because we all were arriving on a certain date and Alex stated he couldn't get there until the next day.

We all arrived in Ft Lauderdale, Florida. We stayed there being that Miami was just across the bridge. We arrived at the hotel and got our room keys. My friends helped me to my room since Alex wasn't there yet. I was pissed. Here I was, doing all this by myself because he wasn't coming until the next day.

I open the door to our room. Something seemed off. There were rose petals and appetizers in the room. That wasn't strange because this is what Alex does. He typically went above and beyond to make things special. Then it happened. He came from behind the door. My smile probably lit up the entire state of Florida. I didn't have to endure the night alone. We too, could be a couple like everyone else. He knew it was important. With him traveling, we missed several couple gatherings.

We had an hour or so before we had to meet his football friend. Everyone retreated to their rooms to settle in. I so much loved and appreciated him for surprising me and always creating an experience for me.

Alex laid down the plan. He had a car coming to take us to meet his college football friends at a hotel in Ft. Lauderdale, and then we would meet back up with the group we came with.

Our transportation arrived. It just happened to be my favorite truck. A black Cadillac Escalade. I thought or assumed it was coincidence. I got in. I was just glad to be with my boo and spend time with each other. We traveled along the A1A beachside until we arrived at a hotel. We get out and Alex said we were meeting them on the rooftop of the hotel.

As we exited the elevator. I heard music. It appeared to be a guy playing the guitar and singing. As I squinted, it looked like I noticed my cousin. You know your family from anywhere. I continued to walk toward the guitarist and realized all our friends were there. I turned around to look at Alex, and he was on one knee. I screamed.

The man I loved took the time to hire a planner and surprised me with the best proposal ever from the hotel rooftop overlooking the ocean. That was the beginning of our fairy tale.

As I told you earlier, I believed God when he told me, I would get everything I wanted.

Romans 8: 28 says it best.
And we know that all things work together for good to them that love God, to them who are the called according to his purpose.

How to Journal Through the Trials of Life

Suffering a loss of any kind can be traumatic and/or devastating. A loss can be due to illness, divorce, incarceration, or drugs. Here are some steps to help you journal through your emotions.

For most of us, it's hard to communicate how we feel after a trauma. A great technique to express how you are feeling is to start a journal of your thoughts and feelings.

When you are having a bad day or going through tough times, or when you are feeling depressed or sad, it's time to journal. Writing your feelings allows you to get things off your chest and helps you to respond and react differently.

1. What's your favorite memories of a loved one?

_____

_____

_____

2. What would my life be like if I didn't lose my loved one?

_____

_____

_____

3. How does life look without your loved one? Describe your new normal.

_____

_____

_____

_____

4. If you are sad or depressed, think or do something that will make you smile or laugh. List them here.

_____

_____

_____

5. Develop habits to strengthen you.
   - Speak I AM affirmations.
   - Develop confidence.
   - Start having a positive attitude.
   - Change how you feel about yourself.
   - Build your self-worth.
   - Work on ways to strengthen your mindset.

What have you done to strengthen your brokenness?

_____

_____

_____

6. Abide in Christ. What does this mean to you?

_____

_____

_____

7. I keep God at the center of everything I do. I know he's with me through every smile and tear. Do you feel God's presence?

_____

_____

_____

8. Talk to God daily and meditate or get in a quiet place so you can hear what your next steps should be. Sometimes I prayed and sometimes I listened. Do you have a place to pray and listed to God? Write or journal your thoughts daily so you can track your high and low points of the day.
Example:
1) Woke up sad

_____

_____

_____

9. Change your thoughts or reset your emotions. If you are having a bad day and can't seem to get past or push through these feelings, then replace thoughts of sadness or bad memories with memories that make you laugh or smile.
10. Do things that make you smile or happy. It makes me smile to dance. Putting on a fun upbeat song and just dancing will change your emotions.
11. Create habits or daily rituals. Pray and read to strengthen your mindset.
12. Recite and learn Bible verses. When the trials of life hit, having scriptures down in your spirit that you've been reciting or meditating on, will give you strength to continue on.

Aha Moment:

CHOOSE to be happy every day. This doesn't mean you won't have sad moments. It means they don't steal your entire day. By resetting your emotions, you add hours of happiness to your day.

About The Author

Stephanie Smith is a shining example of what it truly means to deny yourself. One day while serving as a leader in the discipleship ministry called MasterLife at Berean Christian Church, Stephanie said to God, "Stretch Me."

What you see before you today used to be a shy, computer programmer who would be perfectly content to sit in a cubicle and do her job. This wife, woman of God, mother, computer programmer, and now author and life coach are the direct result of that one simple prayer request, "Stretch Me."

Stephanie believes in paying it forward in helping women who struggle to overcome life trials, get UnStuck. She also believes in the process she calls relationship rehab, where she teaches singles to get their fairytale. Once they get it, she teaches them how to be wise and have a lasting marriage by leading with love.

Stephanie earned her bachelor's degree in computer science in 1991 from Orlando

Business College and has worked for more than 25 years as a computer programmer. She has served at Berean Christian Church in Stone Mountain, GA in the Masterlife and Discipleship Ministry.

Stephanie married her high school sweetheart at the age of 20. She gave birth to her son Ryan, who as a very young child died of a cancerous brain tumor. Later Stephanie gave birth again and is the proud mother of a beautiful daughter, Autumn.

After going through a lengthy divorce and now living her new normal, she embraced re-building herself and was determined to be an example to her daughter of how to win in life, love and business.

Stephanie and her husband Alex are living out their fairytale and enjoying their life together in Atlanta, GA with their four incredible children.

NOTES

Made in the USA
Middletown, DE
19 May 2019